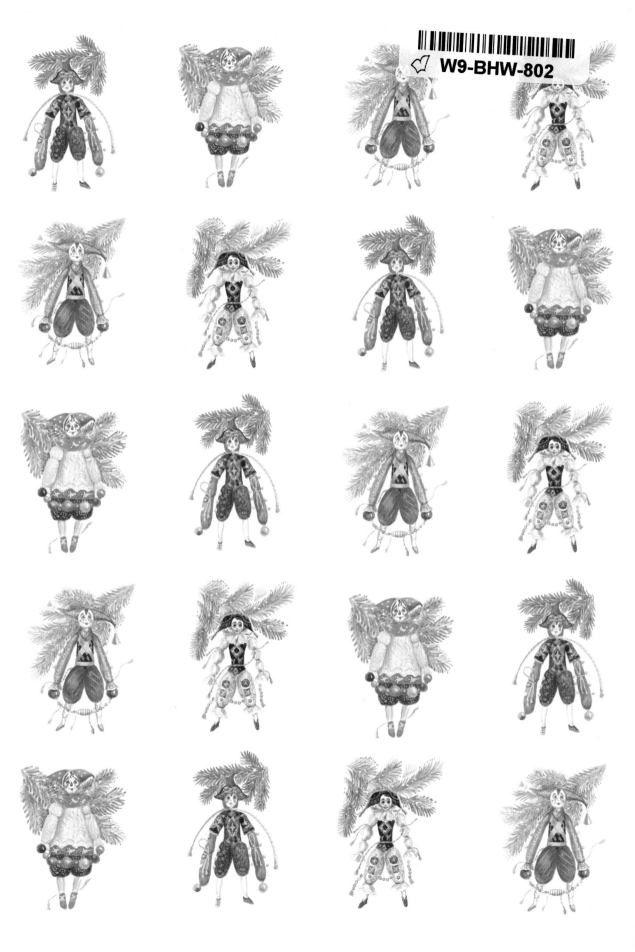

Moscow Ballet's® GREAT RUSSIAN Nutcracker

by
E.T.A. Hoffman

A Poetic Re-telling of the Story by
Vladimir Kostrov

Illustrated by
Valentin Fedorov

Adapted from Russian into English by
Mark Herman and Ronnie Apter

Concept by
Akiva and Mary Talmi

Moscow Ballet
Pittsfield, MA

Library of Congress Control Number: 2003109065

Kostrov, Vladimir

Moscow Ballet's Great Russian Nutcracker/E.T.A. Hoffmann; a poetic re-telling
of the story by Vladimir Kostrov; illustrated by Valentin Fedorov; adapted from
Russian into English by Mark Herman and Ronnie Apter; concept by Mary
and Akiva Talmi; Illustration: Valentin Fedorov; Design: Robin O'Herin;
Project Coordinator: Dmitri Yudanov

ISBN 0-9743082-0-X

Now, **little book,** we will tell a tale of long ago and far away, told in the music of wizards and fairies, told in beautiful stormy melodies, full of wonder and enchantment.

Our story begins on Christmas Eve at a merry ball in Russia. Here are Masha, her parents, and her brother Fritz—now there's a merry mischief-maker!

Masha and Fritz watch wide-eyed with excitement as their parents welcome guests from far and near, lovely ladies and elegant gentlemen who whirl and twirl like a world in motion, while excited children rush to presents under a glittering Christmas tree.

But still awaited by all is he who dresses in clothes of olden times, Drosselmeyer, poet, sorcerer, and Masha's own godfather, master of magic and childhood dreams. Here he is!

And what has he brought?

Puppets! Dolls! Harlequin and Kissy,

and Masha's favorite, a sturdy Nutcracker, an
amazing present!

Proud nose, a smile, big eyes, pigtail tucked
beneath a German hat.

What a funny doll! A true artiste—best in
the world at cracking nuts.

How the crowd of children rejoices as the Nutcracker, ever ready, by the merest flip of a finger, cracks a shell in its sturdy teeth. Hear the happy cries of boys and the laughter of the girls as the Nutcracker breaks and splits nut after nut after nut after nut. It is, apparently, nothing to him—his jaws are hard, hard as granite. And Masha clasps him to her heart and thanks her godfather Drosselmeyer.

Listen now to the fairy tale of the Nutcracker Drosselmeyer told to amuse the children: —Down in the cellar's darkness and dampness was the home of the Queen of Mice.

In the gloom she bore a son, the Mouse King with a hairless tail. He could not bear this great embarrassment, and so resolved always to destroy all the toys of happy people.

As his evil mother instructed, he planned to wreak a terrible vengeance: all dolls to crack, all soldiers to break, all cakes and pastries to devour utterly. But, instead of winning his furious war, he was defeated in hard-fought combat, vanquished by a fairy-tale Prince.

Yet, though the first battle may be over, other battles still await us, for the evil Queen took cruel revenge and cast a spell on the noble Prince. What that was and what will happen is a tale as yet untold.

Thus the Magician finished his story. Now the children turn to their presents and the magical tree lights up at last.

But that Fritz, the mighty warrior, decides to carry off the Nutcracker, and to everyone's sorrow, the little boy breaks the doll. And Masha sobs, full of grief, and rails at her brother: you naughty boy! Don't you know the world believes that a good heart is always best? In stories and life, being foolish or clever is nothing next to the inner beauty of kindliness and sympathy.

Later, without her parents and friends, Masha is in her room with her toys.
Through the large window spills the moon's magic mysterious light.

The light shows Masha sleepily cradling the broken Nutcracker in her arms. As she consoles him, the toys, the flowers, the pictures start to come alive.

Masha by now is sleeping and dreaming. Spurred by a star flying through the firmament, the miraculous fir tree grows and grows and underneath it resolute Fritz has set up his soldiers row on row.

The Mouse King once more takes on the role of frightener and biter and toy destroyer. He leads into battle, from under the fir tree, his disgusting detachments of horrible mice.

Off runs Fritz! Masha is trembling. The mice have numbers, the soldiers honor. Is that enough to protect Masha? But lo! the Nutcracker rises to join them, bravely attacking the enemy.

Goodness fights on the side of freedom; evil endorses slavery! The mice are scattered! Masha is rescued! Oh, daring Nutcracker! God be with you! Though the battle seethes, your motto stands: Who takes up a sword against us by the sword shall be taken down!

The loathsome Mouse escapes by flight into the rotting basement dust.
May all such tyrants be defeated! May peace and freedom rule the Earth!

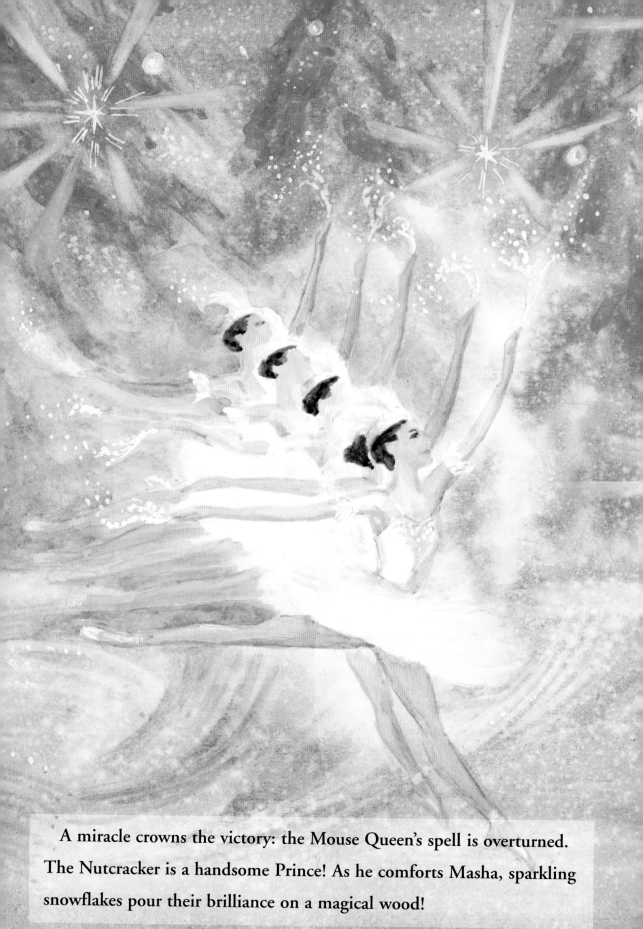

A miracle crowns the victory: the Mouse Queen's spell is overturned. The Nutcracker is a handsome Prince! As he comforts Masha, sparkling snowflakes pour their brilliance on a magical wood!

A sleigh appears to take the couple through the trees of the hushed and white Snow Forest to the Land of Peace and Harmony.

Some are in song, some are in story, some are simply asleep, but all of us dream about this Land. Its people, unbowed by sorrow, follow their visions, and every language is understood. Here the Dove of Peace and pristine angels joyously greet the happy pair.

Here people of every race and country welcome Masha and the Prince.
Here men and animals dwell in peace.

But even here the loathsome Mouse intrudes and the Nucracker Prince
forcefully responds. The Mouse King, stripped of his spiteful role, forever
leaves the scene!

And now the whole world starts to dance. Impassioned Spanish rhythms sound as castanets click and guitars thrum. Rather than fight, the bulls strum and bestow on Masha the gift of daring.

An Arabian dance weaves its ancient pattern like sand flowing
along the dunes. Elephants sway and watchful lions tap on drums.
The elephants, too, have a gift for Masha. Theirs is wisdom.

Messengers from the Yangtze, the Chinese river, rush in dancing, like butterflies, watched by a celebrated dragon, who may himself have fluttered onto the scene with another gift: playfulness.

Bewitching ballet is Russia's glory, today, tomorrow, and evermore. Her talented bears pluck balalaikas. The gift that they bestow is strength.

Bordeaux, Nantes, Paris, Marseille conclude
the review in a carousel of flying feet and
swirling skirts. French unicorns bow violins as
children lead in gentle lambs with one last gift
for Masha: kindness.

The land of Peace and Harmony dances, and
snowflakes and the glowing moon, by whose
beams dragons and bears and elephants whirl
and all the lights of village and city swirl together
with loving Masha and her Prince.

And, setting the standard of earthly beauty, living flowers begin to dance.
Multi-colored crowds are circling and each good heart calls to itself: Farewell,
old New Year's tale, farewell; may fortune promise another meeting.

The melodies, dances, and loyal love will last forever in our passionate hearts. Parting truly is sweet sorrow as the magical sounds fly off and fade. Farewell, farewell, the ballet echoes. Farewell Hoffmann and Chaikovsky, poet and composer whose names, I know, you too will not forget.

Farewell, old New Year's tale, farewell; may fortune promise another meeting. I know that come another year I shall pass this way again!

In a blink, sleep flies from Masha. Around her are Drosselmeyer, her parents, and Fritz. Two tears are in her bright blue eyes and the Nutcracker doll in her hands.

Moscow Poet Vladimir Andreyvich Kostrov was born in Russia in 1935. A graduate of Moscow State University, Kostrov edits *New World* magazine and is director of the International Pushkin Committee. He won the *All Russia Poetry* and *Gold Calf* awards in 1987, the *Moscow Mayor* and *Tvadrovski* awards in 1998, the *Bunin* award in 2000. He is a three-time winner of *Russia's Song of the Year* award. Kostrov's lyrics are featured in the music of Muradeli, Pakhmotova, Kvint. He wrote the libretto for the opera *Jordan.*

Illustration: Valentin Fedorov draws on a unique set of influences to create the colorful sets and puppetry of Moscow Ballet's Great Russian Nutcracker. He was born in Ibresi in the Chuvash Republic. He is a graduate of the famed Moscow Artistic Academic Theatre, founded in 1898 by Stanislavsky and Nemirovitch-Danchenko, and a protege of the legendary Valery Leventhal of the Bolshoi Ballet. Since 1988, he has been the art director at the Chuvashia State Theatre of Opera and Ballet. He has designed more than 40 productions including *Sylvi* (1990), *La traviata* (1992), *Rigoletto* (1999), *Marriage of Balzaminov* (1991), *Cupper Horse Rider* (1993), *Swan Lake* (2000), *The Nutcracker* (2001), *Bayaderka* (2002), the puppet theater production *Ruslan and Lyudmila* (1996) and the drama *Restless Sophia* (1998). In 1991, his *Blackberry Along the Fence* was the winner of the *Best Performances of Russia Festival.* In honor of his contributions to theatrical design, he was given the title *Honored Artist of Chuvashia.*

Akiva Talmi's producing credits include *Moscow Ballet's Great Russian Nutcracker;* Glasnost Festival; the Cynthia Gregory Tour, First Lady Nancy Reagan, Chairperson; and *From Bolshoi to Broadway,* starring Valentina Kozlova. He created and booked the Godunov tour, and *From the Top and Carnival* TV specials with Violette Verdi and Itzak Perlman. Talmi (B.S. and M.A., Juilliard School) has composed feature film scores for *TWO, Longest Journey* (Columbia) and won the *Richard Rodgers, Leonard Bernstein,* and *Metropolitan Opera Guild* awards.

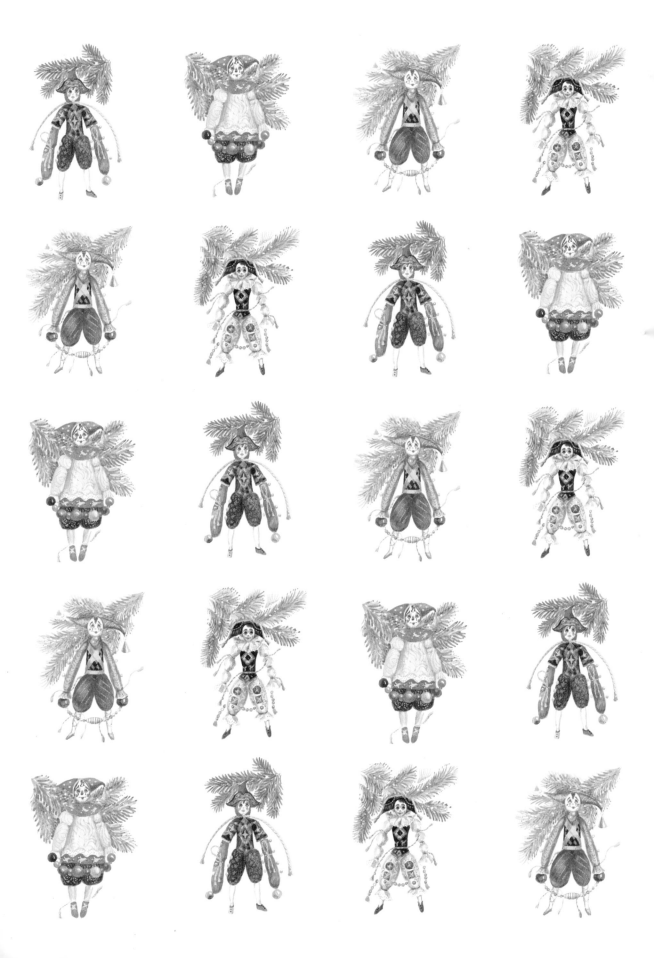